To: _____
From: _____

MW00416378

Published by Sourcebooks, Inc.
P.O. Box 4410, Naperville, Illinois 60567-4410
(630) 961-3900
Fax: (630) 961-2168
www.sourcebooks.com

ISBN-13: 978-14022-0848-5
ISBN-10: 1-4022-0848-0

Printed and bound in the United States of America
SP 10 9 8 7 6 5 4 3 2 1

Kiss Me

coupons

XXX

Kiss Me

c o u p o n s

Present this coupon for a long,
sensuous kiss in the rain.

Kiss Me

c o u p o n s

With this coupon, I will recreate the scene of **our first kiss** for you, and kiss you just the way I did then. ♥

Kiss Me

c o u p o n s

✕✕✕

Let's kiss like we're in the final scene of a movie about an epic love affair!

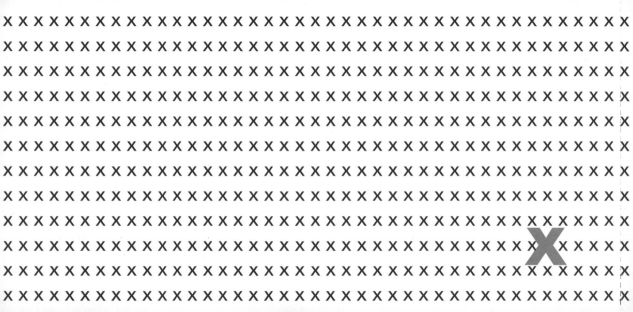

Present this coupon and
I'll kiss you anywhere
you'd like.

♥

KISS ME

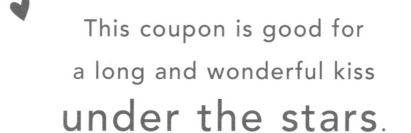

This coupon is good for
a long and wonderful kiss
under the stars.

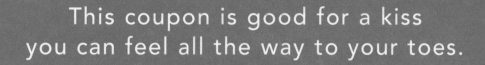

This coupon is good for a kiss
you can feel all the way to your toes.

Let's enjoy a prelude to a kiss:
we'll stand very close,
our mouths not quite touching,
and we'll see who can hold out
the longest before starting a kiss.

♥

Kiss Me

coupons

This coupon is good for one experimental kissing session—anything goes.

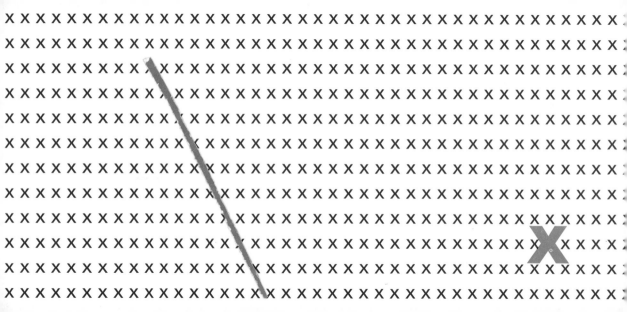

Let's try to keep a straight face while we kiss like porn stars—in public!

KISS ME

This coupon is redeemable for one **ecstatic kiss** in a high place, with the world at our feet.

Kiss Me
coupons

Let's kiss near a body of water—the tide will guide our rhythm.

When you redeem this coupon, lie down and close your eyes—I'll surprise you with a kiss...somewhere!

♥

Kiss Me

c o u p o n s

Let's kiss with nothing touching but our lips
until we can't stand it any longer.

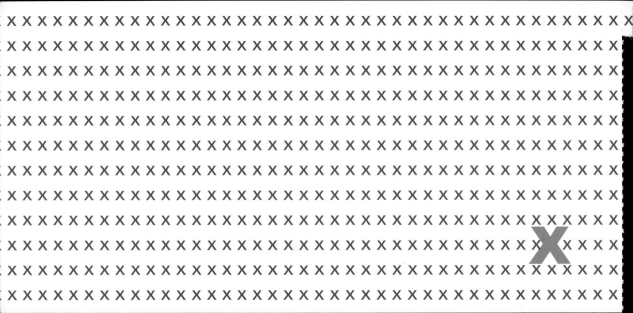

This coupon is good for

a sweet holiday kiss

under the mistletoe!

♥

KISS ME KISS ME KISS ME KISS ME KISS M
KISS ME KISS ME KISS ME KISS ME KISS M
KISS ME KISS ME KISS ME KISS ME KISS M
KISS ME KISS ME KISS ME KISS ME KISS M

KISS ME

KISS ME KISS ME KISS ME KISS ME KISS M
KISS ME KISS ME KISS ME KISS ME KISS M
KISS ME KISS ME KISS ME KISS ME KISS M
KISS ME KISS ME KISS ME KISS ME KISS M

With this coupon, we'll enjoy
a long, leisurely kiss
outdoors with the sun shining
on our faces.

Kiss Me

coupons

xxx

This coupon is redeemable for
one penetrating, no-nonsense,
searing kiss.

Redeem this coupon for
a sensuous kiss
on the back of the neck.

♥

Kiss Me

xxx

coupons

With this coupon, I will gently kiss every part of your face and throat, ending with your lips.

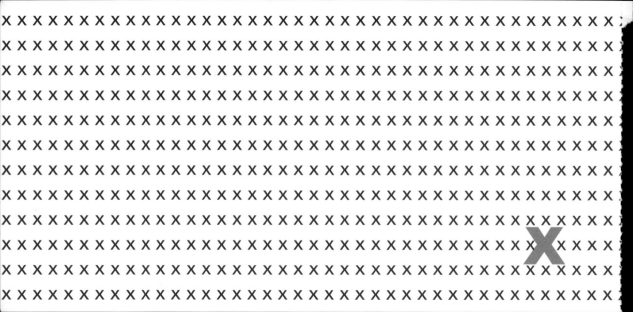

Redeem this coupon for

a wild, stormy,

passionate kiss

full of fire and music.

♥

Redeem this coupon after a long day:

it's good for one warm hug

and as many soft kisses

as you need.

Kiss Me

coupons

Let's play your favorite song and kiss in time to the music.

Let's spend the day together
and no matter what we're doing
or where we are we'll stop to kiss
each other every thirty minutes.

♥